That kind of door

That kind of door

Alan Finlay

ISBN 978-0-9870282-9-7
ebook ISBN: 978-1-928476-25-2

Deep South
contact@deepsouth.co.za
www.deepsouth.co.za

Distributed in South Africa by
University of KwaZulu-Natal Press
www.ukznpress.co.za

Distributed worldwide by
African Books Collective
PO Box 721, Oxford, OX1 9EN, UK
www.africanbookscollective.com/publishers/deep-south

Deep South acknowledges the financial assistance of
the National Arts Council for the production of this book

NATIONAL ARTS COUNCIL
OF SOUTH AFRICA

Cover design: Liz Gowans and Robert Berold
Text design and layout: Liz Gowans

Cover painting: 'Detail of a wall' by Quinten Edward Williams

Versions of some of these poems have appeared in *Illuminations* and
New Coin. I would like to thank the poets and friends who have
encouraged my work in different ways over the years. And for their
help with this book: Kobus Moolman, who read an early version of
the manuscript, and Robert Berold for his insight, patience, and the
grounded editorial/shaping process.

for david & jonah

flavia, bianca

Contents

I. The door

II. Here

III. There

IV. The longing

I. The door

The other son

One son came into the room, his eyes all red with aching.
He looked at me as if i was still there.

I said: But I am here.
He said: But you *won't* be when you're there.

The other son shifted corrugated tin
across his head

to slide out the light. I called and called and called
like a wolf at his door: Let me in, let me in –

He set a fire to the stone chimney, and made the cold wait.

I went across the river to him; he was all legs.
He was still stretched out, the way you do in sun:

everything about him said.
I waited.

I watched him rake the earth.
I watched the sky bless him.

Wall

He put his arm through the wall.
He punched a hole through the glass.
He put his arm through the wall.
The glass cut wide like a belt buckle.
He put his arm through the wall.
The water keeps flooding.
You could see the white of fatty cells.
His arm trapped there, half poking out
Without language.
Still.

door

I want to give my son a door,
to hang across his
far room, something to open

to close.
Something to start.

a dark door
a light door, a

door painted red.
It doesn't matter,
a door, with hinges

open, close

keep lightly shut
slam. open
again
            that

kind of door.

For our fire

Something blue washed through me into your fire.
Sparks hissed up, waist high –
it wasn't water, it was paraffin

and the flame leaped back onto both of us
collecting us, scorched children of the night
lying beneath leaves, the offering stars

as they whispered to us: *you are already there.*
There is no risk in taking love into
your body, letting it burn, a paraffin lamp

or a twisting veldfire set alight by wind
or shrapnel, glass. The risk is letting it burn
so no-one knows

calling the wind back to the surface of
the sea. The risk is listening to those
who do not believe in burning.

And when the black sacks of smoke lisp
above this earth: they will find that we were here.

II. Here

At the *café de las letras*

At the *café de las letras*,
the old men float behind glass
with maps on their heads.

They are turning bread
to soil, a passing
remark, about duties

families, or politics
into another
silence, another pause

for water, thinking of
a weak bladder, or what's
left for lunch.

Conversation is passed
between them, soft
as someone's hand.
                    One reads
a municipal
bill, shifts it back

knowledgeably, explains
how totals are
calculated. The other

will not give up
on his contempt; it's what
he has.
        Later, he
will go and pay
complain again.

                    Start
another story. Another asks
to join the conversation

and plunges
into the obscurity
of small print. Is

left that way, in the bright
elevator of his

look. The conversation
meanwhile
has spilled in another direction,

to the study of birds. There is
no use quarrelling
about geography, except

why this land
is yours. The man
in the *marrón*

jersey laughs, lights
a fire, against a cold
wall; the other

is on page two
of the newspaper. He checks
the time, glances

at the day outside.
Tomorrow, the third
man, quiet, until now

might have something
to say. Their winter

jackets hitched
on the back of the chairs,
coffee, half drained.
               Perhaps he
will look through

the shadows of his
spectacles, and notice
a difference.
               Perhaps

he will arrive late, or
leave early, angry
at something. He talks

suddenly, turning
his hands as if winding
a skein

of wool around his index
finger. It is red wool,
or a tired blue.

The one
who has been
studying the fine print,

moves his lips
across the rim of the glass
like a pulped book

curling gnocci

You press a thumb
lightly down the ribbed
palette – not too

hard down on the
dough, but firm
enough so it

curls into a snail.
Then you boil
it like any

other thing. like
crabs, like eggs or
potatoes

this gnocci set out on the
kitchen table in a
wasteland of flour

as your mother
slices dough cleanly

away from her.

You use:

mashed potato
egg
salt, flour
"so it's already cooked"

then when you
boil it
if it floats

it's not ready, you wait

on the rib
of the kitchen
chair

like you did
as a teenager,
in frayed denim

shorts
remember
how you sat

this way
bubbling over
to your sisters

in competition in deep love

as i practise quietly
to get the curls
right

press not too hard
hard

enough   to make
this inch

of mashed

potato, salt, egg and
        flour

into something
        that can
be understood.

Wings

She has a child. She has a child, close to the rain
and in an apartment in Pergamino
as the rattle of a morning bus pours
its yellow across her window,
                    she holds
this child, tells this child, lets this child go.

Single mother: rainy footsteps, on the way
to family, *kinder*
working hard to keep things close.
                    While outside
the day pours, the rain
pours. The sun, the work pours.

She hates rainy days. She likes the sun.
she says: why do i work so hard
why is it i cannot stop?

She scowls at the doves that nest on her patio.
she takes her laptop,
                    she takes her child
dresses her. Says: now you are a bird
and the child cries when there are no wings.

                    Somedays
her family arrives, with fresh stories
and the baby. She holds him like a bell, cooing
like the doves, listening to the ringing
in her ears.
                    Her brother fixes
the shower. They exchange differences, samenesses.
They share Coke, *factura*.

They hug and kiss and go home.
            her child

is tired now. She rocks her
on her lap, says: *te amo, bueno.*
            And then

becomes a hawk
            hovering above
            a field –

            and the chase begins, mother, mouse
            around the apartment

until the child checks
her back for wings,
where there are none, and cries

            inconsolably again.
            Today

you are not my mother,
she says, determinedly,

as if this magic might work.

Today, you are still my daughter,
her mother replies,

and yesterday, and tomorrow –
now, *dormir.*

Si, the child says,
            collapsing finally,
            in her bed

what's the use
        of wings anyway
                if we cannot fly
                        together, *mamá*?

Porque

Why. There is no answer. *Porque*

si. Porque no. Just pick up the
phone, uncertain cigarettes, just

pick up your bag, your purse, the
shingle of the keys, *campera*!

Quieres zapatos. No. Pull that zip
right up to the ceiling. Hood

on, pink. Go out into the rainy
day, a hand run down a back, this

way. You can't say no. Why.

To change what is hidden
in history.
From those
who will not say.

Why? We pull like oxen
over the rim.
We go, because we go.
We die, right here, in a field of white tulips

Lagos 772

in the dark tinsel
    of this street
      outside the apartment
         – *Lagos 772*, she spells
      the numbers out loud –
and then it starts
        the stamp and dance
            and hugs in the
      cold – *tengo frio*
a shiver through the wolf
        as we stand
or sit,
        and wait
           for *abuela*
           y melisa
        to arrive

        for school.
            still

        night, in this blue
      street,
        the handstands of
      streetlights flickering

           off,
              then
          on,   like a lost

        confidence – but here,

there is no
afuera
    afuera before
        or after,

       and this is not
      even
sadness –

    the stamp
      of cold, the early
  cars through the after
  rain,
     the spilt

streets
    awash
      at the end of *Lagos*
  772

Long-distance

my son on the skype
screen, looking
rad
boss, he said, my hair this
way

it's different i said,
just longer he said
And then he took me outside

to show me the garden,
where his mother had dug
the pond into the soil

and spread the lilies. The garden's
looking great
he said
at last, i said.
What? he said, but i think he heard me.
Is the doorhandle

fixed? I asked
no he said,
and when you are alone, what do you do
I latch it
he said.

The crossing

We are building something here,
first chance. Make it good, love.
Let's build the decking to the ship

we want to float, unhitch the sails
trapped on the mast, let go the birds
in all their detail – love, we are building ships

for us to travel. Let's stay, let's
make this plan work, divide the map
let's make the map divided work in pairs

love, let it happen, go
let it happen language, a hurt, a scar
lost signal between two cellphone towers. What earth

drags us here, flies us here, with stitches on
my throat, with fingers through my hair, my love
will this be the other side with you

accept this

accept this crushed response, this toe's
fixed artery, this love with
its heavy throat, this fear, this anxiety

accept this: open door, closed against
the cold, winter heaving like a lung
accept this, closed door, lung without a sky

all these rooms
take them into you, make room for another
room beside the one you keep for me.

III. There

through these streets

and you,
    my son broken,
        splintering

            ash
        you my
            son
                with awkward
                  drums
                    where are you
                          hurrying to.

Amongst the fathers

I watched him play
the rugby match –

the same gawky stride,
thinner than I imagined
him, last time I saw him

the same decisive
uncertainty going
into the maul

the same willingness
to follow
direction, to have it straight

the same hesitant
outspokenness
chastising another player

to be a part
of the team, to fit in

I thought he looked
vulnerable

with his thin
white legs, and his
angled determination.

It took me a while

to recognise him
I don't know if he saw

me standing there. I
thought that maybe

he did, amongst
the other fathers

scattered along the
sidelines.

I went up to him

after the match. He was red, sweaty
still complaining
to another boy.

Someone greeted
me with "sir", then shifted

to the side, as if to
let me in. I stood beside him

as he bent
down to do something
with his tog bag, I was right there: standing next to him

I said: "Hello." Firmly,
questioning.

He didn't look
up, he said: "Jesus" or something
he didn't look at me at all

stood up
and walked
away

wait for him

i.

I have lost my child. He is
strong. He
has roots, he knows

how to bake in windows.
He has
steel, growing wildly

into the earth. He has
delicate patterns like tendrils

on the wall. He has a sky
he has, these

footsteps, now bone
now

ii.

Wait for him, to come
round here, hands

hitched in pockets,
smile like

tin crumpled
in a fire.

No use telling
him. Or even

asking;
no point saying
        you can

see it in his
felled anger; in the clutch

of his
temples; you can see

it in his
angled roots, the stiff way

he walks down to
the water.

IV. The longing

Passport photo

he looks up through the water
his eyebrows narrowed, acidic
his jaw clenched to hide the
teeth he said are going skew again
his eyes two taut muscles
daring you to fight, you father
he knew would get the picture
for the travel documents.
and where will I put him,
with all that
rage?
In my wallet?

Letter

Unpeel the
skin, wrapped
around this house

hardening to
a callus
do not let

the heart grow
numb
in the current here

write a postcard
write a letter
let him take a letter

opener and
rip open the pig-heart
of that letter.

I can hear your voice darkened

I can hear your
voice, darkened

resist, pulling
back
into the shadows as if to

finally say:
it is me deciding.
And I feel this way

which is not
how you expected

me to feel. I was
calling to you
out to you saying

please let this
be the way it
was. And you were saying

it has already
changed, gone.

mopani

i.

uncertain windows
where do i go

my child
on the edge of the willows,
low in the water,

what does he see
that I cannot see?

As he watches
through the binoculars
his throat contorted, dry

until the scratching thorn
bleeds him into shade

until the water
comes, pouring

> *father father*
> *where are you going,*
> *why are you leaving me*

And what use
are these

hands, with my
son gone?

What can they hold
like "truth"
a word I have used

insistent, awkward,
"the truth is"

place it on the table
where we argue
again

the crocodile
will not
move. The elephant

on the ledge of
water, darkly
shakes its trunk

stamps the
concrete on
the bridge.

One of them has
to cross
to the other

side.

ii.

the bird
the guide explained
whose name I

forget the bird
is a sign of water

and when the fire
comes to their
collapsed eggs

they lift the water
they, all of them
on their wings

like so many leaves,
to douse the hiss
of eggs

I watched
the vultures
        through

        the heat,
        looking for
        a kill, something

        final, something
        certain, bloated

        hissing
        Something to say.

                        I saw
                        their heads
                        in the dry air

iii.

How can we go

carefully, skittish as buck, to the water's edge?

iv.

      the snap of
heat, in branches

crowding a heavy room;
      elephant footsteps,

through the riversand

who has been
here?

v.

    The bull is in
charge;
Ears pinned back against the ringstone

        one eye
gored to close,

turns to face
the car, edges its shadow
closer

vi.

We cross the bridge slowly
the water black beneath us
as we gibber   wafer
birds in the heat of the car.

We don't stop for
elephants anymore.
Their eyes gelled
inside their skulls.
Their whiff of stiffened skin
musked by shit and gallons
of piss.

You just cry,
frustrated, hide your face
in a book of animals

don't you feel I love you dad?

            I shift
from my smoking place
where sun-shrikes
thread the

gland of a stream
make way for the
sweeper's
broom,

as she switches
the leaves from the place
where i was standing.

You watch me from the
verandah of the
Mugg & Bean, waiting
for our pancakes.

I want to say:

See how dark the birds fall
catch the light!
See how their glittering

empties itself of longing –

vii.

                and
                      your singing
                  is ripping
through thorn, the birds

There is a sadness

that blows both ways, both ways
do you hear me?

One wing lifted, the other one
tethered, do you hear me?

This ton of steel, this way.

It burns up, and it goes
down. Do you hear me, now? I am calling.

There is one way to leave this earth.
There is another way to return.

Do you hear me, plans gone wrong?
Mr Plans Gone Wrong.

An open door. You can leave
anytime. Or forget again.

A closed door, your heart
scratched out with pencil lead.

Oh, that thickening. That running,
that going, that going forever

a child, returning

In the anarchy
     of what is
         harvested here,

      locusts knitted
    in the grain.

        In the energy of the mule
          that pulls
             the plough, slicing the

               parallax,
          through fields
     we may know.

In the curt
     shoulders of
     a child, returning
       from rugby, red-faced
        scruffed
     a bruise
         where he got hammered
           on his cheekbone.

        In the red spines
           of these letters, dissolving
           What remains. To be forgotten.

        What shadow? What

           hand. What can
             we eat?

Noah's madness

No more crying, if you want to make this work.
Be tough on yourself
like a hammer is tough on a nail.
Hah hah
hammer in the world.
It won't come begging.

And when the song of the elephant's wrung.
the whisper of the snake
the tiger's hiss
and pawing of the mute panda
the white ant encapsulated in the lava of its sac.

The ampersand spills out the amnion.
Uncurls into another letter.
It stands up on two legs
and bows like an "h"
before the master.

And oh god, oh god oh god the rain
Claws against the hills
when words come down to earth
to dust,
a son's
dry lips
on skype.

The school tie

i showed him how to knot
a tie
he practised and i
straightened it, a mirror.

then later his friend taught him
another trick,
and he preferred that saying
this is neater

dad, this is not a knot
of water, or how to kill
a snake,

or a long road that goes nowhere

so i have to close it
off with thorn-tree
branches.

it nests neatly
at his throat, this new
school tie

his friend showed him
how to
knot.

A key in the night

He is asleep now. When he wakes
he will gather his toys, and gather his
Strength, and find something

else to do. He is awake now,
he is thinking of sleep,
but there is too much keeping him here.

He balances this feeling
like a ball. He shows me
in the garden
insists the way a child turns

a key in the night,
The way a child reaches up
on the crunches
of his toes – he shows me

in the darkening garden how
he can open the door.
                              The sun
is turned sideways against
his skin.

We change direction
pointing north, so I can see the cricket ball.
Tiny as it is, against the sun

Blackened
As it is
in the sun's wax.

When he wakes
he finds himself here.
He can't shake himself loose of the sand,

The water blows through his skin
This is how I swim, the whale says
This is the way the water is flowing
the sea says

The whale's teeth are half a grin.
It turns, sideways, so the boat knows.
It runs itself ashore
It is dangerously close to the water's edge.

When he wakes, the wolf is running
Already

Back into the night
clipped close to the forest
its tail white as paper
its eyes glittering like school stars

Do you have to go? he says again
in a voice quiet as a silo,
tight as a piece of grain.

He is awake and his father is going

perhaps, he thinks, what is a father anyway
I will show you, he says.
I do not want to resent you, he says.

he pulls himself together
with bits of string, Prestik, regression
And then holes in his pocket

The shell of his tablet
where he rocks, pressing keys
into mystery

The sky can be bright as Bluetooth
The road, narrow as one leg
The dark garden quickening

He is awake, in another world

The sea is flowing one way
The wind is burning this way
North is at the end of the road,
It returns
And licks him like a wolf.

He is awake, and the father goes
is still going
a going that pours
silver back into the wound.

To that sea

that crashes erasing everything
returns and takes another breath
to that splashing sand – to that wind

that howls against the legs,
to that bush
that particular thorn,
those clouds eloping

that green sea, that faraway – the drill of distant ships
if i could close these arteries of longing – i would.
If I could rearrange this,

forever. this
distance. This try. If I could
go back to where it begins, where

love begins, the hurting sea,
the life that poured into me. if i could
remember each swollen step,

say hear me, hear me

I want to read a poem

that is
about sky, but
this kind
of sky.
This
blue
that is
stone,
    turned
unturned, that is
smooth as the
surface
of skin. I want
to read this
poem, language
where all
else fails.
as the father
takes away,
as the mother
takes
away. This
stone,
between
mother and
father.
This star,
this
sky. Where the glands
of birds
float, in channels
of heat, so high,

rest there in the
boeing currents
a poem
of earth
returning, as it
never was.
I want to
read a poem,
la tierra,
the terror
this earth
to let all things go
unbound
the love, let all things go
I want to
return, to this
poem, this door,
this unawakened
earth, where
ploughs are set to.
All this dark earth
all this wasted exhausted
all this
impossible,
snow

stuck in San Nicolás

in a hotel
with her
daughter, the
rain

broken
road, away
from
home

flavia,

who lives
in the eye
of the wolf,

who is a road
back
a road
so blue, flooded

Printed in the United States
By Bookmasters